Readings and itineraries

1

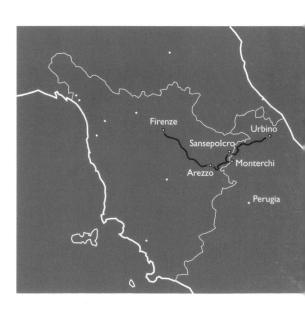

Firenze

Urbino

Sansepolcro

Monterchi

Arezzo

Perugia

ISBN 88-86392-50-8
© 1998 s i l l a b e s.r.l.
piazza Damiano Chiesa, 49 - 57124 Livorno
tel. 0586.867034 - fax 0586.869119

managing editor: *Maddalena Paola Winspeare*
graphic design: *Laura Belforte*
editing: *Federica Lehmann*
translation: *Anthony Cafazzo*

photolithography: *La Nuova Lito - Florence*

photographs: *Remo Bardazzi, Marco Rabatti*

Raffaele Monti

Readings and itineraries

Piero della Francesca

From the
*Triumphal Diptych
of the Lords of Urbino*
to the
Flagellation

s i l l a b e

The triumphal Diptych of the Lords of Urbino

We begin our itinerary at the Uffizi, where we find the *Triumphal Diptych of the Lords of Urbino (Dittico trionfale dei Signori d'Urbino)*, one side depicting the *Triumph of Battista Sforza* and the *Triumph of Federico da Montefeltro*, while portraits of Battista Sforza and Federico da Montefeltro appear on the other.

Originally, the two portraits were framed together and made up a sort of portable diptych that could be opened and closed like a book. The Poggio Imperial inventory of 1652, apart from erroneously identifying the two personages as Francesco Petrarca and Laura, also indicates that the two leaves were mounted in a frame which was "hinged together". This is borne out, amongst other evidence, by the better state of conservation of the inner portion. However, already in 1692 they were found within "a partially unframed, wholly gilded ornament". The current frame dates back to 1835. Since 1773 the work has been held by the Uffizi Gallery, and only in 1834 were the two personages identified correctly.

4

QVE MODVM REBVS TENVIT SECVNDIS ·
C. ONIVGIS MAGNI DECORATA RERVM ·
· LAVDE GESTARVM VOLITAT PER ORA ·
CVNCTA VIRORVM ·

CLARVS INSIGNI VEHITVR TRIVMPHO ·
QVEM PAREM SVMMIS DVCIBVS PERHENNIS ·
FAMA VIRTVTVM CELEBRAT DECENTER ·
SCEPTRA TENENTEM ᴓ

CLARVS INSIGNI VEHITVR TRIVMPHO ·
QVEM PAREM SVMMIS DVCIBVS PERHENNIS ·
FAMA VIRTVTVM CELEBRAT DECENTER ·
SCEPTRA TENENTEM ⁊⸗

QVE MODVM REBVS TENVIT SECVNDIS ·
CONIVGIS MAGNI DECORATA RERVM ·
LAVDE GESTARVM VOLITAT PER ORA ·
CVNCTA VIRORVM ·

The history of this work, together with its structural singularity and perfection of form, arising whence the artist's mind turns to divination of the visible, make it arduous to fully grasp its import, despite the accuracy of its current state of museum conservation. In fact, the exceptional 19th C frame accentuates the painting's fragmentation into four distinct images, so that overall, the diptych gives the impression of a small lay altar, dismantled and reassembled in alien surroundings.

The painting, as can be deduced from the decorations on both its sides, had been conceived of as a work in isolation, to be placed in a practically empty space. This is also confirmed by the small dimensions of the original frame which bore the hinges uniting the two tablets. Only by reconstructing this frame — a trying task indeed — would we be able to measure the original distance separating the two portraits. At present, this distance can only be appreciated on the other half of the painting (the *Triumph of Battista Sforza* and the *Triumph of Federico da Montefeltro*), thanks to the perfect continuity of the countryside in the background, just barely interrupted at the center.

This said, there however remains the main, as yet unsolved, problem of the painting's mobility and the unfolding sequence of its various components, an unfolding which no sort of museum display could ever do justice to. In fact, the artist designed it so that the first "leaf" to come into sight would be the *Triumph of Battista Sforza*, in which the wagon and its right-to-left motion establish the movement of opening the 'page', which, in turn, reveals the inner portion of the diptych containing the two ducal portraits. The desired effect is a sequence presupposing a wholly private viewing, unfolding in at least three discrete episodes.

If it is therefore impossible for a museum to reproduce the unfolding that della Francesca had intended, it is equally unthinkable that we could ever restore the work to that private space – a studio or bedroom – which the artist had in mind when he created it.

The diptych's two images are united by the same internal light source from the right serving to set it apart from the surrounding, randomly-lighted environment.

Keeping the foregoing in mind, let us now go on to a 'reading' of the painting, respecting the sequence of the four images.

First of all, the lower portion depicts a tombstone, on which the virtues of Battista Sforza, second wife of Duke Federico, are illustrated. The first line of the inscription, "QUE MODUM REBUS TENUIT SECUNDIS", attests to the fact (stressed by the choice of the past "tenuit", meaning "maintained") that the painting was executed after the death of the Duchess in 1472, the year that art historians almost unanimously attribute the work to.

Then, above the tombstone a road is brought to view in the foreground by the thinning out of the stones, thus revealing the advancing triumphal wagon. Battista is sitting reading, flanked by two theological virtues; two other virtues are seated on the borders of the wagon, which is drawn by two unicorns and driven by Love. This last figure constitutes a sort of *trait d'union* between the chaste eroticism symbolised by the unicorns and the black rendition of Charity, which carries a pelican in its lap, symbolising the sacrifices of maternal love (Battista died in childbirth). The horizon in the background opens afar and each figure in the triumphal group appears outlined by the varying contour of the hills.

QVE MODVM REBVS TENVIT SECVNDIS ·
CONIVGIS MAGNI DECORATA RERVM ·
LAVDE GESTARVM VOLITAT PER ORA ·
CVNCTA VIRORVM ·

The first image which appears on the 'book's opening' is that of Battista. Here the effect of a 'luminous whole' makes up the portrait's emotional backbone. The flawless profile melds with the background running behind the figure, though the vast countryside's sole purpose is to isolate the Duchess' head even further from the boundless expanse of sky beyond. This 'medal-like' profile was chosen by della Francesca — perhaps in the wake of Pisanello — precisely in order to accentuate the commemorative theme of the work. On the other hand, this layout is one of the two privileged perspectives with regard to the stereometric measures of the human head which della Francesca himself describes in two pages of his treatise, De prospettiva pingendi (ff. 81r-82v). The contours enclosing Battista's profile determine a volumetric rotation which can be perfectly inscribed in a sphere where the depth plane and foreground are just barely hinted at by the celestial radiance. The limits of the profiling 'follow' the rotation of the volume, which appears immersed in a sphere whose depth and emerging planes are regulated by the celestial light.

Pisanello, Medallion of Malatesta Novello, *bronze, c. 1445, Paris, Musée du Louvre.*

This sort of "great vitreous phial" (Roberto Longhi), due precisely to the unfolding, twisting and cascading of the pearls, appears in perfect syntony with the structure of the bust enveloped in the shadow of the countryside. Even the winding of her hair about the jewel on her head is intensified by the incredible mass of folds behind it. This fixes the image to the left, while at the same time imparts an imperceptible motion which, thanks to Battista's translucent countenance, projects the entire volume towards the image of the Duke. The subtle tension, upheld by the meditative, inward glance evident on the face of the Duchess, serves the purpose of focusing on the amplification of Federico's proportions, an effect which is further accented by the curved line of his hat.

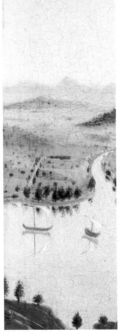

The artist uses the continuity of the horizon and the contiguous line formed by uniting their chins to fix the equilibrium between the two portraits, an equilibrium which is well reflected in the fact that Federico, Duke and husband, emanates no 'brilliance', but is uniformly enveloped by it. The painter is thus allowed the possibility of expressing the natural signs of human physiognomy: wrinkles, the shadowing of the bone structure and so forth.

It is therefore evident – and this became immediately apparent after the last, splendid restoration – that the luminous substance in which the figures are embodied becomes gilded in the portrait of Federico.

The deeply meditative and heroic character of the Duke arises, in fact, from the opaline reflection of Battista, from a "mental and loving power", that is to say, from the same figurative unfolding, and not from the two gazes encountering each other in a geometric line. Thus, the 'amplification' of the male figure does not, in the end, appear disturbing; it does not modify the overall balance in the least. Perhaps, even the coursing waters at the bottom right serve to indicate this continuity of path.

Finally, closing the diptych brings into view the *Triumph of Federico*. Here the theological virtues guide the wagon being drawn by white horses, while the triumphant Federico is crowned by Victory, in an overall composition in perfect symmetry with that of the *Triumph of Battista*.

From the whole of the work, the luminous force of the portraits seems to be inversely proportional to that of the Triumphs. In fact, while this luminous power is presented as stronger in the ethical-heroic *Triumph of Federico*, in that of his recently-deceased spouse, the radiance, including that of the unicorns and Virtues, is slightly dimmed.

An itinerary: from Florence to Urbino

Above:
Autoportrait, *detail of the fresco series on the* Legend of the True Cross, *Arezzo, Church of San Francesco.*

The Diptych is the only work by della Francesca in Florence. Therefore, as no other traces of della Francesca's work remain in the Tuscan capitol – though memorials may abound – it is left to the visitor to follow the course of his work in Umbria and the rest of Tuscany. It is a moving, unrepeatable experience which for nearly a century has revealed the greatness of this artist.

Travelling up the Arno River nearly to its source, and then continuing as far as Perugia and Urbino, one can appreciate the signs of his artistry in the courts of these small cities, rather far from the usual tourist itineraries. Here we will find some of the highest achievements in western figurative art, as well as testimony to that which Jacob Burckhardt would have defined as the oneness of life and meditation.

Church of San Francesco in Arezzo

Going back to the origins of Piero della Francesca's work, in the Church of San Francesco in Arezzo, we find the great fresco composition, the *Legend of the True Cross*, which was completed in 1466 and partially restored recently. These frescoes represent the heart of the artist's achievements, not only because they occupy a central point in his career, but above all because it is the only figurative "complex" by della Francesca that is left to us. Taken together, they bear exhaustive witness to the new manner of expressing perspective, the path through, and the harmonic measures within, a space that allows the observer to perceive the dynamics of both the internal and external structures of the representation. The work blends the aim of recounting the legend of the 'True Cross' with that of calling forth Christians to the Crusades against the Turks after the fall of Constantinople. Those who wish to undertake a 'reading' of this extraordinary page in our figurative history should take into account the degree to which the 'rule' and the path through the images were conceived by della Francesca as a reflection of a universal vision. It is a conception which is emphatically visual and emotional – the splendour of the countryside comes to mind – but which, in order to understand fully, must be identified with its ultimate substance, namely, the power of modern man to define and vary the rules of representing the world.

What results is an extremely exacting pictorial manner, stretching from perfection of harmonious permutation to the 'material' of painting itself. In essence, we find ourselves face to face with the essence of the so-called "light painting", altogether capable of delineating perfect volumes in space, without however depriving body or landscape of that light by virtue of which – as we have already seen with regard to the diptych – they stand out as bodies in space.

Solomon's encounter with the Queen of Sheba, *detail of the fresco series on the* Legend of the True Cross, *Arezzo, Church of San Francesco.*

Arezzo Cathedral

Still in Arezzo, this time in the Cathedral, we find *Magdalene*, encumbered and in part curtailed by the famed Tarlati tomb (1783). This fresco, dated rather uncertainly to about 1452, or 1466 or later, though defined in an apparently random space, exerts an extraordinary power of attraction by virtue of the precise and volumetrically perfect relation that links the gaze to the arm lifting the hammer. Thus, this latter almost seems to fulfil the role of closing within a lighted space the opening through which the pleats of the dress can be discerned.

Magdalene, *fresco,*
190 × 80 cm, Arezzo,
Cathedral.

Monterchi

If we continue towards the source of the Arno River, we come to the hill-top town of Monterchi, where we can find another renowned della Francesca masterpiece, *The Madonna of Childbirth (Madonna del Parto)*, which renews the miracle and attractive power of this new formal measure. Probably painted before 1467, the most recent restoration, scholastically 'philological', has unfortunately robbed this masterpiece of the top of its circular framework which, though repainted, nonetheless respected the original structure of the work. Moreover, its current debatable placement thwarts any attempt at understanding even the distance at which the work should be viewed. Thanks to recent research, we now know that the iconography of the pregnant Madonna was not all that rare in those times, and that only with the advent of the Counterreformation did this subject become explicitly taboo.

Madonna of Childbirth, *before and after recent restoration, detached fresco, 206 × 203 cm, Monterchi.*

Sansepolcro

Resurrection of
Christ, *mural,
fresco and tempera,
225 × 200 cm,
Sansepolcro,
Pinacoteca Comunale.*

Opposite page:
Polyptych of Mercy
(*"Polittico della
Misericordia"*),
*painting on wood
panel, 330 × 273 cm,
Sansepolcro,
Pinacoteca Comunale.*

Saint Jerome, *fresco
detached from the
apse of the Church
of Sant'Agostino
in Sansepolcro,
130 × 105 cm,
Sansepolcro,
Pinacoteca Comunale.*

The town of Sansepolcro lies just a few kilometres beyond Monterchi. It is here that the painting, the *Baptism of Christ* (*Battesimo di Cristo*), long considered by critics, beginning with Longhi, to be the first known work of della Francesca, had been kept until 1857, first in the Priory of San Giovanni Battista, and then later in the Cathedral (1807). The tempera on wooden plate was sold in 1857, and since 1861 has been housed in the London National Gallery. Scholars are still rather divided over the dating of this work: some, among whom Longhi, are inclined towards 1440, while others maintain as late as 1460 to 1465.

Today the walls of the Palazzo Comunale (now the Pinacoteca) of Sansepolcro are adorned with della Francesca's *Resurrection of Christ* – a fresco widely recognised as the painter's greatest masterpiece. Apart from the *Resurrection*, which probably dates back to 1459, the Pinacoteca also houses an extremely important, albeit small, collection of della Francesca's work, whose culmination is represented by the *Polyptych of Mercy* (*Polittico della Misericordia*, 1454-55). This masterpiece, which had long remained dismantled,

28

can be seen today in reconstructed form, though in a frame unworthy of the work's structural and spatial relationships.

Also worthy of note in this same museum is the fresco fragment which was discovered in 1955 and comes from the apse of the Church of Sant'Agostino. Two years after its discovery, it was detached from the supporting church wall, which was destroyed in the process. It can be dated to after della Francesca's Roman sojourn, from 1458-59. Although its current location cannot do justice to the work's dimensions or the direct relationship that the fresco's original arrangement could establish with the viewer, it has the advantage of highlighting the intense gaze which concentrates the entire nucleus of the work's formal excellence.

The Madonna of
Senigallia, *oil on
wood panel, 61 × 53.5
cm, Urbino, Galleria
Nazionale delle
Marche, Palazzo
Ducale.*

Urbino

Now at the borders of Tuscany we approach the source of the Tiber River, which in itself marks another fundamental passage in della Francesca's work, his Roman 'period', of which, unfortunately, no trace remains. Disregarding the superb Perugian altar-piece, the *Polyptych of Saint Anthony* (*Polittico di Sant'Antonio*), we arrive at the city of Urbino to admire the two masterpieces on display at the Palazzo Ducale: the *Senigallia Madonna* (*Madonna di Senigallia*) and the extremely intellectual *Flagellation*. Here, it is at last possible to understand the culmination of that 'climate', which, still vibrant long after the crucial undertakings of della Francesca, would be transmitted through his disciple, Giovanni Santi, and eventually induce Raffaello d'Urbino a few decades later to repropose throughout Europe a transformation of the artistic experience of Piero della Francesca: in Rome, Raffaello, the "*Sommo Urbinate*" (Supreme Citizen of Urbino), accepts the charge of painting the renowned Papal *Stanza della Segnatura*, which at the time still contained frescoes by Piero della Francesca.

The Flagellation, painting on wood panel, 58.4 × 81.5 cm, Urbino, Galleria Nazionale delle Marche, Palazzo Ducale.

Chronology

1430	Works in Sansepolcro
1437-1438	Works in Perugia
1439	Works in Florence
1445	Stipulates contract for the *Polyptych of Mercy*
1445-1450	Works in Ferrara, Le Marche and Loreto
1448	Replaces Bicci di Lorenzo in executing the frescoes of San Francesco in Arezzo
1450	Visits Rome
	Saint Jerome
1451	Works in Rimini where he carries out the frescoes *San Sigismondo and Sigismondo Pandolfo Malatesta*
	Paints the central portion of the *Baptism of Christ*
1452-1455	Completes San Francesco frescoes
1455	Recalled to complete *Polyptych of Mercy*
	The *Flagellation*
1458-1459	Resides in Rome while working on the Vatican frescoes
1460	*Portrait of Sigismondo Pandolfo Malatesta*
	The *Polyptych of Sant'Agostino*
1465-1466	Completes the frescoe series on the *Legend of the True Cross*
1468	Paints the standard of Arezzo
1469	Stays in Urbino as the guest of Giovanni Santi
	The *Polyptych of St Anthony*
1470	Dedicates his treatise on perspective to Federico da Montefeltro
1469-1472	The Montefeltro altar-piece
1472 circa	*Nativity* for the chapel of Franceschi (now in the London N.G)
1473	The *Uffizi Diptych*
1475 circa	The *Perugia Polyptych*
1475-1476	The *Senigallia Madonna*
1492	Buried in family chapel

Bibliography

R. Longhi, *Piero della Francesca*, Rome 1927, expanded edition in *Opere complete*, vol. III, Florence 1963.
A. Focillon, *Piero della Francesca*, [1934-1935], Paris 1952.
K. Clark, *Piero della Francesca*, London-New-York 1969².
E. Battisti, *Piero della Francesca*, Milan 1971.
C. Ginzburg, *Indagini su Piero*, Turin 1981.
L. Bellosi (ed.), *La pittura di luce. Catalogo della mostra*, Florence 1990.
A. Paolucci, *Piero della Francesca. Catalogo completo*, Florence 1990.
C. Bertelli, *Piero della Francesca*, Milan 1991.
Several conferences and shows were held by the "Centro Piero della Francesca" on the occasion of the five hundredth anniversary of the artist's death.

Printed October 1998
by MediaPrint, Livorno
for
sillabe